Quantitative Methods in Business Research: A Practical Guide

Rizwan Raheem Ahmed, Ph.D.

DEDICATION

This book is dedicated to my Late Mother and Father who have provided me the financial, emotional, and Parental opportunities to raise me, provided higher education and supported me in my initial professional life journey.

TABLE OF CONTENTS

ACKNOWLEDGMENTS

I Acknowledge my wife who has supported me during writing this book. She has also helped me to generate book cover and other relevant material on Photoshop. She has encouraged me all the way in my journey.

CHAPTER 1: INTRODUCTION

Purpose of the book

The purpose of this book, Quantitative Methods in Business Research: A Practical Guide, is to provide a comprehensive overview of the most commonly used quantitative research methods in business research. This book is specially designed for business researchers who need to conduct rigorous and effective quantitative research to inform business decisions and strategies.

The book covers a wide range of topics, including research design, data collection and analysis, statistical inference, and hypothesis testing. It also provides step-by-step guidance on how to use statistical software such as SPSS and Excel to analyze data and generate insights.

The primary goal of this book is to help business researchers develop a solid understanding of the quantitative research process and the core statistical concepts that underpin it. By doing so, they will be better equipped to design, execute, and interpret the results of quantitative research studies.

The book also emphasizes the importance of using quantitative research methods in conjunction with qualitative research methods, as both approaches have unique strengths and limitations. By combining the two, researchers can gain a more holistic understanding of the research topic and generate more robust insights.

Overall, the purpose of this book is to demystify the often-complex world of quantitative research and provide business researchers with practical tools and techniques they can use to conduct high-quality research that can inform critical business decisions. Whether you are a seasoned researcher or just starting out, this book is a valuable resource that will help you navigate the complex world of quantitative research and achieve your research goals.

Importance of quantitative methods in business research

Quantitative methods are a crucial aspect of business research, allowing researchers to collect and analyze data in a systematic and objective manner. Quantitative research methods are particularly useful for investigating relationships between variables, testing hypotheses, and making predictions.

One of the primary benefits of using quantitative methods

in business research is the ability to collect large amounts of data that can be analyzed using statistical techniques. This enables researchers to identify patterns, trends, and relationships that may not be apparent through qualitative research methods.

Another key advantage of using quantitative methods is their ability to provide objective, measurable results. Quantitative research is based on numerical data, which can be analyzed using mathematical formulas and statistical models. This allows researchers to make precise measurements and draw conclusions based on objective data rather than subjective opinions.

Quantitative research methods are also useful for testing hypotheses and making predictions. By using statistical models and techniques, researchers can test the validity of their hypotheses and make predictions about future outcomes based on the data they have collected.

In addition to these benefits, quantitative research methods are also useful for identifying cause-and-effect relationships between variables. By analyzing data using statistical techniques, researchers can identify factors that are likely to affect the outcome of a particular business decision and make informed choices based on this information.

Overall, the importance of quantitative methods in business research cannot be overstated. By providing objective, measurable results and enabling researchers to test hypotheses and make predictions, quantitative methods are an essential tool for anyone conducting research in the business world. Whether you are a business researcher or simply interested in learning more about quantitative methods, this book provides a practical guide to using these methods effectively in your research.

Overview of the book

The book "Quantitative Methods in Business Research: A Practical Guide" is written for business researchers who want to learn how to use quantitative methods in their research. The book covers a wide range of topics, including survey design, sampling methods, data analysis, and statistical inference.

The book begins with an overview of the research process, which includes defining the research question, selecting the research design, and identifying the data sources. The authors then discuss the importance of survey design and explain how to develop effective surveys that can provide reliable and valid data. They cover topics such as question wording, response options, and scale development.

The next section of the book focuses on sampling methods. The authors explain the different types of sampling methods, including probability and non-probability sampling, and provide guidance on how to select the appropriate method for a given research project. They also discuss sample size determination and provide practical advice on how to calculate the sample size needed for a study.

The book then moves on to data analysis, covering topics

such as descriptive statistics, correlation analysis, and regression analysis. The authors provide step-by-step instructions on how to conduct these analyses using popular statistical software packages such as SPSS and Excel. They also provide guidance on how to interpret the results of these analyses and how to present the findings in a clear and concise manner.

The final section of the book covers statistical inference, which is the process of making generalizations about a population based on data from a sample. The authors explain the concepts of hypothesis testing and confidence intervals and provide practical guidance on how to conduct these procedures.

Overall, "Quantitative Methods in Business Research: A Practical Guide" is a comprehensive and practical guide for business researchers who want to learn how to use quantitative methods in their research. The book is written in an accessible and engaging style and includes numerous examples and exercises to help readers apply the concepts and methods discussed in the book.

CHAPTER 2: UNDERSTANDING QUANTITATIVE RESEARCH METHODS

Definition of quantitative research methods

Quantitative research methods are a set of procedures and techniques that are used to collect and analyze numerical data. These methods are commonly used in business research to generate numerical data that can be used to make informed decisions. This subchapter will de ne the quantitative research methods that are commonly used in business research.

Quantitative research methods are designed to generate numerical data that can be analyzed using statistical methods. These methods are used to identify patterns, trends, and relationships between variables. They are also used to test hypotheses and to evaluate the effectiveness of interventions.

The main types of quantitative research methods used in business research include surveys, experiments, and observational studies. Surveys are used to collect data from a large sample of individuals, while experiments are used to test the effects of a particular intervention. Observational studies are used to observe and measure the behavior of individuals or groups.

Quantitative research methods also include data analysis techniques such as descriptive statistics, inferential statistics, and multivariate analysis. Descriptive statistics are used to describe the characteristics of a sample, while inferential statistics are used to make inferences about a population based on a sample. Multivariate analysis is used to analyze the relationships between multiple variables.

Quantitative research methods have several advantages over qualitative research methods. They are more objective, reliable, and precise. They also allow for the measurement of complex concepts and the testing of hypotheses.

In conclusion, quantitative research methods are a set of procedures and techniques used to collect and analyze numerical data. These methods are commonly used in business research to generate data that can be used to make informed decisions. The main types of quantitative research methods include surveys, experiments, and observational studies. Data analysis techniques such as descriptive statistics, inferential statistics, and multivariate analysis are also used in quantitative research.

Types of quantitative research methods

Quantitative research is an essential technique used in business research to gather and analyze numerical data. This type of research is useful when researchers aim to measure and quantify the relationships between different variables. There are different types of quantitative research methods used in business research, and each of them has its unique characteristics and purposes. In this chapter, we will explore some of the most common types of quantitative research methods used in business research.

1. Survey Research

Survey research is one of the most popular types of quantitative research methods used in business research. It involves the use of questionnaires or surveys to collect data from a sample of individuals or organizations. The survey questions can be structured or unstructured, and they can be administered in different ways, such as face-to-face, online, or via telephone. Survey research is useful when researchers aim to collect data on attitudes, opinions, behaviors, or demographic information.

2. Experimental Research

Experimental research is a type of quantitative research that involves the manipulation of one or more variables to observe the effect on another variable. It is useful when researchers aim to establish cause-and-effect relationships between different variables. In experimental research, the researcher manipulates the independent variable and measures the effect on the dependent variable.

3. Correlational Research

Correlational research is a type of quantitative research that involves the measurement of the relationship between two or more variables. It is useful when researchers aim to determine the degree of association between different variables. Correlational research does not establish causality, but it can provide valuable information on the strength and direction of the relationship between variables.

4. Longitudinal Research

Longitudinal research is a type of quantitative research that involves the collection of data over an extended period. It is useful when researchers aim to observe changes or trends in variables over time. Longitudinal research can be either cross-sectional or panel study.

5. Descriptive Research

Descriptive research is a type of quantitative research that aims to describe the characteristics of a particular phenomenon or population. It is useful when researchers aim to provide a detailed account of a specific issue or topic. Descriptive research can be conducted through surveys, observation, or secondary data analysis.

In conclusion, there are different types of quantitative research methods used in business research, and each of them has its unique characteristics and purposes. The choice of the research method depends on the research question, the type of data needed, and the available resources. Business researchers need to select the appropriate research method to ensure the validity and reliability of their research findings.

Advantages and disadvantages of quantitative research methods

Quantitative research methods are widely used in the business world to analyze data, test hypotheses, and identify patterns and trends. These methods involve the collection and analysis of numerical data, which can be analyzed using statistical techniques to draw conclusions and make predictions. While quantitative research methods have many advantages, they also have some disadvantages that researchers need to be aware of.

Advantages of Quantitative Research Methods

One of the biggest advantages of quantitative research methods is that they are objective. Since the data collected is numerical, it can be analyzed using statistical techniques that are not subject to personal biases or interpretations. This makes it easier to draw accurate conclusions from the data and to make informed decisions based on the results.

Another advantage of quantitative research methods is that they allow for large sample sizes. This means that researchers can collect data from a large number of participants, which can help to ensure that the results are representative of the population as a whole. This is particularly important in business research, where decisions may have far-reaching consequences.

Quantitative research methods also allow for greater precision and accuracy. Because the data is numerical, it can be analyzed using statistical techniques that can reveal patterns and trends that may not be immediately apparent. This can help researchers to identify important insights and make more informed decisions.

Disadvantages of Quantitative Research Methods

One of the biggest disadvantages of quantitative research methods is that they can be limited in scope. Since the data collected is numerical, it may not capture the full range of experiences and perspectives that people have. This can limit the insights that researchers can gain from their data and make it difficult to draw valid conclusions.

Another disadvantage of quantitative research methods is that they can be time-consuming and expensive. Collecting and analyzing numerical data often requires specialized equipment and software, which can be costly. Additionally, analyzing large amounts of data can take a significant amount of time, which can delay the results of the study.

Quantitative research methods can also be limited by the quality of the data that is collected. If the data is incomplete or inaccurate, it can skew the results of the study and make it difficult to draw valid conclusions. To ensure that the data is high-quality, researchers need to take care to collect data in a systematic and consistent manner.

Conclusion

Quantitative research methods have many advantages for business researchers, including objectivity, large sample sizes, and precision. However, they also have some disadvantages, such as limited scope, time and expense, and the potential for low-quality data. By understanding the advantages and disadvantages of quantitative research methods, researchers can make informed decisions about which methods to use in their studies and how to interpret the results.

CHAPTER 3: RESEARCH DESIGN
AND DATA COLLECTION

Research question and hypothesis

Research question and hypothesis are critical components of any research study, including business research. They guide the researcher in identifying the problem, collecting and analyzing data, and drawing conclusions. In this subchapter, we will discuss how to develop a research question and hypothesis that will guide your business research.

A research question is a clear and concise statement that identifies the problem or issue you want to investigate. It should be specific, measurable, achievable, relevant, and time-bound. Your research question should be focused on a particular aspect of the business environment and should be feasible to investigate through data collection and analysis. For example, if you are interested in investigating the factors that contribute to employee turnover in a particular company, your research question could be, "What factors contribute to employee turnover in Company X?"

Once you have identified your research question, you can develop a hypothesis. A hypothesis is an educated guess about the relationship between variables in your study. It is a statement that can be tested through data collection and analysis. A hypothesis includes an independent variable, a dependent variable, and a predicted relationship between the two variables. For example, if your research question is about the factors that contribute to employee turnover, your hypothesis could be, "Increased job satisfaction leads to decreased employee turnover in Company X."

Developing a hypothesis is an important step in the research process because it provides a framework for collecting and analyzing data. It allows you to focus your research e orts on specific variables and to test the predicted relationship between those variables.

In conclusion, developing a clear and concise research question and hypothesis is critical to the success of any business research study. They provide a roadmap for your research, guiding you in identifying the problem, collecting and analyzing data, and drawing conclusions. By following the guidelines outlined in this subchapter, you can develop a research question and hypothesis that will guide your business research and lead to valuable insights.

Sampling techniques

Sampling techniques are an essential part of any business research study. They allow researchers to collect data from a smaller group of individuals or businesses that represent a larger population. This subchapter will explore the different sampling techniques that can be used in business research and their advantages and disadvantages.

The first sampling technique that we will discuss is simple random sampling. This technique involves selecting a random group of individuals or businesses from the population being studied. The advantage of this technique is that it ensures that every member of the population has an equal chance of being selected. However, the disadvantage is that it may not be representative of the population as a whole.

The second sampling technique is stratified random sampling. This technique involves dividing the population into subgroups or strata and then selecting a random sample from each stratum. The advantage of this technique is that it ensures that each subgroup is represented in the sample. However, the disadvantage is that it can be more time-consuming and costly than simple random sampling.

The third sampling technique is cluster sampling. This technique involves dividing the population into clusters or groups and then selecting a random sample of clusters to study. The advantage of this technique is that it can be more efficient than other sampling techniques, especially when the population is geographically dispersed. However, the disadvantage is that it may not be as representative as other sampling techniques.

The final sampling technique is purposive sampling. This technique involves selecting individuals or businesses based on specific criteria, such as their expertise or experience. The advantage of this technique is that it can be useful when studying a specific population. However, the disadvantage is that it may not be representative of the population as a whole.

In conclusion, there are various sampling techniques that can be used in business research. The choice of sampling technique depends on the research question, the population being studied, and the resources available. Researchers should carefully consider the advantages and disadvantages of each technique before selecting the most appropriate one for their study.

Data collection methods

Data collection methods are the backbone of any research project. It is essential to choose the right data collection methods to ensure the accuracy and reliability of the research results. In this chapter, we will discuss the various data collection methods commonly used in business research.

Surveys

Surveys are the most popular data collection method used in business research. Surveys can be conducted through various mediums like online, telephone, mail, or face-to-face interviews. Surveys are an effective way to collect data from a large number of respondents. However, the accuracy of the results depends on the quality of the survey questions.

Interviews

Interviews are another popular data collection method used in business research. Interviews can be conducted in-person, over the phone, or through video conferencing. Interviews are useful when in-depth data is required from a small sample size. Interviews are time-consuming and require skilled interviewers to ensure the accuracy of the results.

Observation

Observation is a data collection method used to gather data by observing people, events, or processes. Observation can be conducted in a natural or controlled setting. Observation is useful when the researcher wants to study human behavior in a particular environment. However, observation can be biased as the researcher may interpret the data differently.

Secondary data

Secondary data is data collected by someone else for another purpose, but it is useful for the researcher's study. Secondary data can be obtained from various sources like government reports, industry reports, company annual reports, and publications. Secondary data is less expensive and less time-consuming than primary data but may not be as accurate or relevant to the study.

Conclusion

Choosing the right data collection method is crucial for any research project. Surveys, interviews, observation, and secondary data are the most commonly used data collection methods in business research. Each method has its strengths and weaknesses, and the researcher must carefully choose the appropriate method for their study.

Reliability and validity of data

Reliability and validity are two critical components of data collection and analysis in business research. Reliability refers to the consistency and accuracy of the data, while validity refers to the extent to which the data measure what they are supposed to measure. In this subchapter, we will discuss the importance of reliability and validity in business research, and the methods used to ensure the data is reliable and valid.

Reliability is essential in business research because it ensures that the data collected is consistent and accurate. When data is reliable, it can be used to make informed decisions and develop effective strategies. There are several methods used to measure reliability, including test-retest reliability, inter-rater reliability, and internal consistency reliability. Test-retest reliability involves repeating a test or survey at different times to determine if the results are consistent. Inter-rater reliability is used when multiple raters are used to score or evaluate data, and internal consistency reliability measures how well the different items in a questionnaire or survey measure the same concept.

Validity is equally important in business research, as it ensures that the data being collected accurately measures what it is supposed to measure. Validity is determined through several methods, including content validity, construct validity, and criterion validity. Content validity involves ensuring that the data collected covers all aspects of the topic being studied. Construct validity measures how well a questionnaire or survey measures the underlying concept, while criterion validity measures how well the data collected correlates with other measures of the same concept.

To ensure the reliability and validity of data, it is essential to use appropriate research methods and tools. This includes using standardized questionnaires and surveys, conducting pilot studies to test the data collection process, and using appropriate statistical methods to analyze the data. It is also important to ensure that the data collected is representative of the target population and that the sample size is sufficient to achieve statistical significance.

In conclusion, reliability and validity are critical components of business research that ensure the data collected is consistent, accurate, and measures what it is supposed to measure. By using appropriate research methods and tools, researchers can ensure that their data is reliable and valid, which can lead to informed decision-making and effective strategies.

CHAPTER 4: DATA ANALYSIS TECHNIQUES

Descriptive statistics

Descriptive statistics are an essential tool for business researchers to summarize and depict data in a meaningful way. These methods provide a clear and concise summary of data that can help researchers gain insights into the underlying patterns and relationships between variables. In this subchapter, we will explore the various techniques used in descriptive statistics and how they can be applied to business research.

One of the most basic methods of descriptive statistics is the calculation of measures of central tendency. These include the mean, median, and mode. The mean is the average value of a set of data, while the median is the value that separates the data into two equal parts. The mode is the value that appears most frequently in the data set. These measures can be useful in identifying the typical or average value of a particular variable.

Another important aspect of descriptive statistics is the calculation of measures of dispersion. These include the range, variance, and standard deviation. The range is the difference between the highest and lowest values in a data set, while the variance and standard deviation provide a measure of how spread out the data is around the mean. These measures can be useful in identifying the degree of variation within a particular variable.

Graphical representation of data is another important tool in descriptive statistics. One of the most common graphical representations of data is the histogram, which provides a visual representation of the distribution of data. Other graphical representations include scatterplots, line graphs, and box plots. These can be useful in identifying patterns and relationships between variables.

Descriptive statistics can also be used to compare different groups or populations. The t-test and analysis of variance (ANOVA) are commonly used techniques in this regard. These methods can be useful in identifying differences between groups and determining whether these differences are statistically significant.

In conclusion, descriptive statistics are an essential tool in business research. They provide a clear and concise summary of data and can help researchers gain insights into the underlying patterns and relationships between variables. By using these methods, researchers can better understand the data they are working with and make informed decisions based on their findings.

Inferential statistics

Inferential statistics is a vital aspect of business research as it enables the researcher to make conclusions about a population based on a sample. It involves using statistical models, tests, and procedures to analyze data and make predictions about a larger group. In this subchapter, we will explore the basics of inferential statistics and how it is applied in business research.

The first step in inferential statistics is to de ne the population of interest. This is the larger group that the researcher wants to make conclusions about. For example, if a business wants to understand the attitudes of its customers towards a new product, the population of interest would be all the customers who could potentially purchase the product.

The next step is to take a sample from the population. A sample is a smaller group of individuals that represent the larger population. Choosing an appropriate sample is important as it must be representative of the population to ensure the conclusions drawn are accurate. In our example, the researcher might select a random sample of customers who have purchased similar products in the past.

Once the sample is selected, the researcher can begin analyzing the data using inferential statistics. This involves using various statistical tests and models to make predictions about the population. For example, the researcher might use a hypothesis test to determine if there is a significant difference in attitudes towards the new product between male and female customers.

Inferential statistics also allows researchers to calculate confidence intervals. These are ranges of values that are likely to contain the true population parameter. For example, if the researcher wants to estimate the average age of all customers who could potentially purchase the new product, they can calculate a confidence interval that is likely to contain the true average age.

In conclusion, inferential statistics is a powerful tool for making conclusions about a larger population based on a sample. It allows business researchers to make predictions, test hypotheses, and estimate population parameters with a high degree of accuracy. Understanding the basics of inferential statistics is essential for any researcher looking to conduct meaningful and impactful business research.

Hypothesis testing

Hypothesis testing is one of the most critical aspects of quantitative research in business. It is a statistical method that helps researchers determine whether a hypothesis about a population is true or not. In simpler terms, it helps to test whether a theory or assumption holds water or not.

The hypothesis testing process begins by formulating a null hypothesis (H0) and an alternative hypothesis (Ha). The null hypothesis is the default assumption that there is no significant difference between two groups or variables. The alternative hypothesis, on the other hand, is the hypothesis that the researcher aims to prove.

To test the hypothesis, the researcher collects data from a sample of the population and performs statistical analysis. The results of the analysis are then used to either reject or fail to reject the null hypothesis. If the null hypothesis is rejected, it means that the alternative hypothesis is true. But if the null hypothesis cannot be rejected, it means that there is insufficient evidence to support the alternative hypothesis.

It is essential to note that hypothesis testing is not a one-time process. In a dynamic business environment, new information comes to light every day, and existing hypotheses may need to be retested. Therefore, researchers must continually review and test their hypotheses to ensure that they remain valid.

There are several statistical tools and techniques that researchers can use to test their hypotheses. These include t-tests, ANOVA, chi-square tests, and regression analysis. The choice of tool or technique depends on the research question, the nature of the data, and the level of measurement involved.

In conclusion, hypothesis testing is a vital component of quantitative research in business. It helps to provide evidence-based conclusions and recommendations that businesses can use to make informed decisions. Therefore, researchers must understand the process and use the appropriate statistical tools and techniques to test their hypotheses accurately.

Regression analysis

Regression analysis is a statistical technique that plays a critical role in business research. It is used to investigate the relationship between a dependent variable and one or more independent variables. Regression analysis is a powerful tool that can help researchers make predictions, understand cause-and-effect relationships, and identify patterns in data.

There are two types of regression analysis: simple regression and multiple regression. Simple regression involves only one independent variable and one dependent variable. Multiple regression, on the other hand, involves two or more independent variables and one dependent variable.

Before conducting a regression analysis, it is essential to ensure that the data is appropriate for the analysis. The data should be continuous, and there should be a linear relationship between the dependent and independent variables. Additionally, the data should be free from outliers and influential observations.

There are several steps involved in conducting a regression analysis. The first step is to determine the appropriate regression model to use. This can be done by examining the scatterplot of the data and determining whether a linear or nonlinear relationship exists between the variables.

The next step is to estimate the regression coefficients using a method such as ordinary least squares (OLS) estimation. OLS estimation involves finding the line of best t that minimizes the sum of the squared residuals.

Once the regression coefficients have been estimated, it is necessary to test the statistical significance of the coefficients. This can be done using a t-test or an F-test. The t-test is used to test the significance of individual coefficients, while the F-test is used to test the overall significance of the model.

Finally, it is essential to assess the goodness of t of the regression model. This can be done using measures such as R-squared, adjusted R-squared, and the residual standard error. These measures provide information about the proportion of variance in the dependent variable that is explained by the independent variables.

In conclusion, regression analysis is a powerful tool that can help business researchers make predictions, understand cause-and-effect relationships, and identify patterns in data. By following the steps outlined above, researchers can conduct a robust regression analysis that provides valuable insights into their research questions.

Correlation analysis

Correlation analysis is a statistical technique that helps business researchers to identify the degree of association between two or more variables. In business research, correlation analysis is used to determine the strength and direction of the relationship between variables. The technique is particularly useful in identifying patterns and trends in data, which can help researchers to make informed decisions.

There are two types of correlation analysis: positive and negative. Positive correlation analysis indicates that the variables move in the same direction, while negative correlation analysis indicates that the variables move in the opposite direction. The strength of the correlation is indicated by the correlation coefficient, which ranges from -1 to +1. A correlation coefficient of 1 indicates a perfect positive correlation, while a coefficient of -1 indicates a perfect negative correlation.

Business researchers use correlation analysis in a variety of ways. For example, they may use it to identify the relationship between sales and marketing expenses. They may also use it to identify the relationship between employee satisfaction and productivity. Correlation analysis can also be used to identify trends in customer behavior, such as the relationship between customer satisfaction and loyalty.

There are a number of factors that should be considered when conducting correlation analysis. These include the sample size, the type of data being analyzed, and the purpose of the analysis. It is also important to consider the limitations of correlation analysis, such as the fact that correlation does not equal causation.

In conclusion, correlation analysis is a valuable tool for business researchers. It allows them to identify patterns and trends in data, which can help them to make informed decisions. However, it is important to consider the limitations of the technique and to use it appropriately. With careful consideration, correlation analysis can be a powerful tool for business researchers.

CHAPTER 5: DATA VISUALIZATION

Graphical representation of data

Graphical representation of data is an essential tool in business research. It is the process of presenting data in a visual format to make it more understandable and accessible. It involves the use of graphs, charts, and diagrams to represent data. This subchapter will explore the importance of graphical representation of data in business research and the different types of graphs and charts that can be used.

The importance of graphical representation of data in business research cannot be overstated. It provides a quick and easy way to understand complex data sets. It allows researchers to identify patterns, trends, and relationships that may not be immediately apparent in tabular data. Graphical representation of data can also help to communicate research findings to others more effectively.

There are several types of graphs and charts that can be used in business research. The most common include bar graphs, line graphs, scatter plots, and pie charts. Each type of graph has its own strengths and weaknesses, and the choice of which type of graph to use will depend on the type of data being presented and the research question being addressed.

Bar graphs are useful for displaying categorical data, such as the number of people in different age groups who purchase a particular product. Line graphs are useful for displaying continuous data, such as the trend in sales over time. Scatter plots are useful for displaying the relationship between two variables, such as the relationship between advertising spending and sales. Pie charts are useful for displaying proportions, such as the proportion of sales attributable to each product line.

In conclusion, graphical representation of data is an essential tool in business research. It allows for the quick and easy understanding of complex data sets, the identification of patterns and trends, and the effective communication of research findings to others. There are several types of graphs and charts that can be used, each with its own strengths and weaknesses. The choice of which type of graph to use will depend on the type of data being presented and the research question being addressed.

Charts and graphs

Charts and graphs are indispensable tools in business research. They allow researchers to present complex data in a visually appealing and easy-to-understand format. The use of charts and graphs helps researchers to communicate their findings effectively to a wider audience, including stakeholders, managers, and decision makers.

One of the main advantages of using charts and graphs in business research is that they can provide a quick, visual representation of data. This can help researchers to identify patterns and trends that might not be immediately apparent when looking at raw data. For example, a line graph can be used to show how sales figures have changed over time, or a bar chart can be used to compare the performance of different products or services.

Another advantage of using charts and graphs is that they can help to highlight key findings and insights. By presenting data in a clear and concise manner, researchers can draw attention to the most important aspects of their research. This can be particularly useful when presenting findings to stakeholders or decision makers who may not have the time or expertise to delve into the details of the research.

There are many different types of charts and graphs that can be used in business research, including bar charts, line graphs, scatter plots, pie charts, and histograms. The choice of chart or graph will depend on the type of data being presented and the research question being addressed. For example, a scatter plot might be used to explore the relationship between two variables, while a pie chart might be used to show the breakdown of sales by product category.

It is important to use charts and graphs appropriately and to ensure that they are accurate and clear. This requires careful attention to detail and an understanding of the principles of data visualization. Researchers should also be aware of the limitations and potential biases of different types of charts and graphs, and should use them in combination with other forms of data analysis to ensure that their findings are robust and reliable.

In conclusion, charts and graphs are essential tools in business research. They can help researchers to communicate their findings effectively, highlight key insights, and make complex data more accessible to a wider audience. By using charts and graphs appropriately and with care, researchers can enhance the impact and credibility of their research and contribute to better decision making in the business world.

Tables and figures

Tables and figures are an essential component of any business research study. They provide a visual representation of the data and findings, making it easier for readers to understand and interpret the results. In this chapter, we will explore the importance of tables and figures in business research and provide guidelines for their creation.

Tables are used to present and summarize data in a structured format. They are particularly useful for presenting quantitative data, such as survey results or financial data. When creating tables, it is important to keep in mind the audience and the purpose of the table. Tables should be well-organized, easy to read, and contain clear and concise headings and labels.

Figures, on the other hand, are used to visually represent data, trends, and relationships between variables. They are particularly useful for presenting qualitative data, such as case studies or interviews. When creating figures, it is important to choose the appropriate type of graph or chart that best represents the data. Common types of figures include line graphs, scatter plots, and bar charts.

When creating tables and figures, it is important to follow best practices to ensure accuracy and clarity. This includes labeling all axes, using appropriate scales, and providing a clear and concise legend or key. It is also important to ensure that the table or figure is referenced and discussed in the text of the research study to provide context and explain its significance.

In summary, tables and figures are important tools in

business research for presenting and summarizing data and findings. They should be well-organized, easy to read, and accurately represent the data. By following best practices for creating tables and figures, researchers can provide readers with a clear and concise representation of their research results.

CHAPTER 6: REPORTING AND PRESENTING RESEARCH FINDINGS

Writing Research Report

Writing research reports is an essential component of the research process. It allows you to communicate your findings, conclusions, and recommendations to others. A well-written research report not only reflects the quality of your research but also influences the decisions of the stakeholders who rely on your work. In this subchapter, we will discuss the essential elements of writing a research report.

The first step in writing a research report is to de ne the purpose and scope of the report. The purpose of the report should be clear, concise, and specific. It should outline the research questions, objectives, and hypotheses that the report aims to address. The scope of the report should also be well-defined, stating what is included and excluded from the report.

The next step is to structure the report. A typical research report consists of the following sections: introduction, literature review, research methodology, data analysis, findings, conclusions, and recommendations. Each section should be clearly labeled and organized logically and coherently.

The introduction should provide background information on the research problem, state the research questions and objectives, and explain the significance of the research. The literature review should summarize the existing knowledge on the topic, identify gaps in the literature, and justify the need for the research. The research methodology should describe the research design, sampling techniques, data collection methods, and data analysis procedures employed in the study.

The data analysis section should present the results of the analysis, using tables, graphs, and charts to illustrate the findings. The findings section should summarize the main findings of the study, highlighting the key results and their implications. The conclusion should provide a summary of the research, highlighting the main contributions and limitations of the study. Finally, the recommendations should suggest practical implications for the findings.

In conclusion, writing a research report is an essential skill for business researchers. A well-written research report should be clear, concise, and well-structured, providing a detailed account of the research process and findings. By following the guidelines outlined in this subchapter, business researchers can effectively communicate their research findings to stakeholders, contributing to the advancement of knowledge in their field.

Presenting research findings

Presenting research findings is a crucial step in any business research process. It allows the researcher to communicate their findings and recommendations to relevant stakeholders. The presentation should be clear, concise, and comprehensive to ensure that the audience understands the research findings and their implications. In this subchapter, we will discuss some tips on how to present research findings effectively.

Firstly, it's essential to understand the audience. Different stakeholders will have varying levels of expertise and interest in the research topic. Therefore, the presentation should be tailored to suit the audience's needs. For instance, if the audience comprises executives who are not experts in the research area, it may be necessary to simplify the language and focus more on the practical implications of the research findings.

Secondly, the presentation should be well-structured to ensure that the audience can follow the ow of information. It's recommended to start with an introduction that summarizes the research question, objectives, and methodology. This helps to provide context and set the stage for the research findings. The main body of the presentation should focus on the research results, including tables and graphs that illustrate the findings. It's essential to explain the significance of the findings and how they relate to the research question. Finally, the presentation should end with a conclusion that summarizes the research findings and recommendations.

Thirdly, the use of visual aids can enhance the presentation and make it more engaging. Tables, graphs, and charts can provide a clear picture of the research findings and help the audience to understand complex data. However, it's essential to ensure that the visual aids are easy to read and understand.

Fourthly, the presentation should be interactive to encourage engagement and participation from the audience. This can be achieved by asking questions, encouraging feedback, and providing opportunities for discussion. Interactive presentations are more likely to be remembered and can lead to more meaningful insights.

In conclusion, presenting research findings is a critical step in any business research process. The presentation should be tailored to suit the audience's needs, well-structured, and use visual aids to enhance engagement. Finally, the presentation should be interactive to encourage participation and lead to more meaningful insights. By following these tips, business researchers can effectively communicate their research findings and recommendations to relevant stakeholders.

Ethical considerations in reporting research findings

Ethical considerations in reporting research findings are essential for maintaining the integrity and credibility of the research. As a business researcher, it is critical to understand the ethical guidelines that need to be followed when reporting research findings. This subchapter provides an overview of the ethical considerations that need to be taken into account when reporting research findings.

One of the main ethical considerations in reporting research findings is ensuring that the research is conducted in an ethical manner. This includes obtaining informed consent from participants, maintaining confidentiality of data, and minimizing harm to participants. Researchers must ensure that the research is conducted in compliance with the ethical guidelines set forth by their institution and relevant regulatory bodies.

Another important ethical consideration is the accuracy and transparency of reporting research findings. Researchers must ensure that the data is accurately reported and that any biases or limitations are acknowledged. It is also essential to be transparent about any conflicts of interest that may exist and to disclose any funding sources.

The ethical considerations also extend to the dissemination of research findings. Researchers must ensure that the findings are presented in a manner that is clear, concise, and easily understandable by the intended audience. This includes avoiding the use of technical jargon and presenting the data in a way that is visually appealing and easy to interpret.

In addition to these ethical considerations, it is also important to consider the potential impact of the research findings on society. Researchers must be aware of the potential implications of their research and consider whether the findings could have negative consequences for individuals or groups. It is important to consider the potential impact of the research and take steps to minimize any potential harm.

In conclusion, ethical considerations are an essential aspect of reporting research findings. It is critical for business researchers to adhere to ethical guidelines in order to maintain the integrity and credibility of their research. By following ethical guidelines, researchers can ensure that their findings are accurate, transparent, and have a positive impact on society.

CHAPTER 7: APPLICATIONS OF QUANTITATIVE METHODS IN BUSINESS RESEARCH

Marketing research

Marketing research is an essential component of any business strategy. It helps businesses understand their customers' needs, preferences, and behaviors. This information can then be used to develop effective marketing strategies that will help the business reach its target audience and achieve its goals. In this chapter, we will explore the importance of marketing research and the different methods that can be used to conduct it.

Marketing research is the process of collecting and analyzing data about consumers, competitors, and the market. It involves gathering information about consumer behavior, preferences, and buying habits, as well as information about the competition and market trends. This information is then used to make informed decisions about marketing strategies and tactics.

There are several methods that can be used to conduct marketing research, including surveys, focus groups, interviews, and observation. Surveys are one of the most common methods, as they allow businesses to gather large amounts of data quickly and efficiently. Focus groups and interviews are also effective methods for gathering in-depth information about consumers' thoughts and opinions. Observation is another method that can be used to gather information about consumer behavior in real-world settings.

When conducting marketing research, it is important to ensure that the data collected is accurate and reliable. This can be achieved by using appropriate research methods and tools, such as sampling techniques and statistical analysis. It is also important to consider ethical considerations when conducting marketing research, such as obtaining informed consent from participants and protecting their privacy.

In conclusion, marketing research is a critical component of any business strategy. It helps businesses understand their customers' needs and preferences and develop effective marketing strategies that will help them reach their target audience and achieve their goals. By using appropriate research methods and tools, businesses can ensure that the data collected is accurate and reliable, and that ethical considerations are taken into account.

Operations research

Operations research is a branch of mathematics that deals with the application of quantitative methods in solving complex business problems. It involves the use of mathematical models, algorithms, and statistical techniques to optimize business operations and decision-making processes.

One of the primary objectives of operations research is to improve the efficiency and effectiveness of business operations. This is achieved by identifying and analyzing the key factors that affect business performance, such as production processes, inventory management, logistics, and supply chain management. Operations research helps businesses to identify the optimal solutions that will maximize their profits and minimize their costs.

Operations research is a useful tool for businesses in various industries, such as manufacturing, transportation, healthcare, and finance. For example, in manufacturing, operations research can be used to optimize production processes, reduce waste, and improve quality control. In transportation, it can be used to optimize logistics and route planning, reduce delivery times, and lower transportation costs. In healthcare, it can be used to optimize patient scheduling, resource allocation, and treatment plans, among other applications.

One of the key advantages of operations research is its ability to provide businesses with actionable insights that can be used to make informed decisions. By analyzing data and developing models, operations research can help businesses to identify the best course of action for their specific needs and goals. This can be particularly useful in situations where there are multiple options or trade-o s to consider.

Overall, operations research is a valuable tool for businesses looking to improve their performance, reduce costs, and increase profitability. By leveraging the power of quantitative methods, businesses can gain a competitive advantage and achieve their goals more efficiently and effectively.

Financial research

Financial research is a crucial aspect of business research, and it involves the study of financial markets, instruments, and institutions. As a business researcher, understanding the principles and methods of financial research is essential for making informed decisions and recommendations.

The primary objective of financial research is to identify and analyze financial data to gain insights into the financial health of a company or industry. This data can be used to forecast future trends, evaluate investment opportunities, and assess risks and returns. Financial research can also reveal opportunities for cost savings and revenue growth.

There are several types of financial research, including fundamental analysis, technical analysis, and quantitative analysis. Fundamental analysis involves examining a company's financial statements, such as its income statement, balance sheet, and cash ow statement, to assess its financial health and potential for growth. Technical analysis, on the other hand, involves studying market trends and patterns to predict future price movements. Quantitative analysis uses mathematical and statistical models to analyze financial data and identify patterns and trends.

To conduct financial research, business researchers must have a thorough understanding of financial markets, instruments, and institutions. They must also be proficient in data analysis and statistical modeling. In addition, they must be able to interpret financial data and communicate their findings effectively to stakeholders.

Business researchers can use various sources of financial data, including financial statements, market data, and economic indicators. They can also use financial research tools, such as financial software, databases, and financial models, to analyze and interpret financial data.

In conclusion, financial research is an essential aspect of business research that involves the study of financial markets, instruments, and institutions. As a business researcher, understanding the principles and methods of financial research is crucial for making informed decisions and recommendations. By using various sources of financial data and research tools, business researchers can gain valuable insights into the financial health of a company or industry and identify opportunities for growth and profitability.

Human resource research

Human resource research is a crucial aspect of business research. It involves the study of the workforce of an organization, their skills, knowledge, abilities, and behaviors. Human resource research is essential for the effective management of employees, recruitment, training, and development programs, and the overall success of the organization. In this subchapter, we will discuss the key concepts and methods of human resource research.

One of the main goals of human resource research is to understand the factors that influence employee behavior and performance. This includes factors such as motivation, job satisfaction, organizational commitment, and leadership effectiveness. Human resource research can also help organizations identify the training and development needs of their employees and design effective programs to meet those needs.

There are several methods that can be used in human resource research, including surveys, interviews, and focus groups. Surveys are often used to gather quantitative data on employee attitudes, opinions, and behaviors. Interviews and focus groups are more qualitative methods that allow researchers to explore in-depth the experiences and perspectives of employees.

Another important aspect of human resource research is the measurement of employee performance. Performance metrics can include objective measures such as sales figures or production output, as well as subjective measures such as supervisor ratings or peer evaluations. Human resource research can help organizations identify the most effective performance metrics and develop performance management strategies that align with organizational goals.

Finally, human resource research can also be used to evaluate the effectiveness of HR policies and practices. This involves collecting data on the outcomes of HR programs and initiatives, such as recruitment and retention strategies, bene ts packages, and training and development programs. By evaluating the effectiveness of these programs, organizations can identify areas for improvement and make data-driven decisions about HR policies and practices.

In conclusion, human resource research is a critical aspect of business research. It provides valuable insights into employee behavior, performance, and the effectiveness of HR policies and practices. By using a variety of methods and metrics, researchers can develop a deeper understanding of the workforce and help organizations make data-driven decisions that support their goals and objectives.

CONCLUSION

Summary of key points

The following is a summary of the key points covered in the book "Quantitative Methods in Business Research: A Practical Guide" for business researchers.

1. Introduction to Quantitative Methods: The book provides an overview of the various quantitative methods available to business researchers, including surveys, experiments, and statistical analysis.

2. Research Design: The book emphasizes the importance of a well-designed research plan, including the selection of appropriate research questions, sampling techniques, and data collection methods.

3. Data Collection: The book provides practical advice on how to collect and analyze data, including the use of surveys, focus groups, and interviews.

4. Data Analysis: The book covers a range of statistical techniques commonly used in business research, including descriptive statistics, regression analysis, and hypothesis testing.

5. Reporting Results: The book emphasizes the importance of clear and concise reporting of research results, including the use of tables, charts, and graphs.

6. Ethics in Business Research: The book discusses the ethical considerations involved in conducting business research, including issues of confidentiality, informed consent, and potential conflicts of interest.

7. Conclusion: The book concludes by emphasizing the importance of quantitative methods in business research, and the need for researchers to stay up-to-date with the latest developments in the field.

Overall, "Quantitative Methods in Business Research: A Practical Guide" is a comprehensive and practical resource for business researchers looking to improve their quantitative research skills. The book provides a step-by-step guide to designing, collecting, analyzing, and reporting research data, and emphasizes the ethical considerations involved in conducting business research. With its clear and concise writing style, this book is an essential tool for anyone working in the field of business research.

Future directions in quantitative methods in business research

The field of business research is constantly evolving, and quantitative methods play a critical role in this process. As technology advances and data becomes more accessible, researchers are presented with new opportunities and challenges. In this subchapter, we will explore some of the future directions in quantitative methods in business research.

One of the most significant trends in recent years has been the rise of big data. With the proliferation of digital devices and the internet of things, businesses have access to vast amounts of data that can be analyzed to gain insights into consumer behavior, market trends, and other critical factors. As a result, data science has become an essential skill for business researchers, and the use of machine learning algorithms and predictive analytics is becoming increasingly prevalent.

Another trend is the growing importance of social media and online reviews. As more people turn to social media platforms to share their experiences with products and services, businesses have an unprecedented opportunity to gather feedback and insights. Social media analytics tools are becoming more advanced, allowing researchers to analyze sentiment, identify influencers, and track trends in real-time.

The use of simulation and modeling is also becoming more prevalent in business research. Simulation allows researchers to test different scenarios and predict outcomes without having to rely on real-world data. This approach can be particularly useful in situations where data is scarce or difficult to obtain.

Finally, there is a growing recognition of the importance of ethical considerations in quantitative methods. As businesses collect more data and use more advanced algorithms, there is a risk of unintentional bias or discrimination. Researchers must be mindful of these risks and take steps to ensure that their methods are fair and ethical.

In conclusion, the future of quantitative methods in business research is bright, with new technologies and techniques emerging all the time. By staying up-to-date with the latest trends and best practices, researchers can continue to make valuable contributions to the field and help businesses make informed decisions.

Final thoughts and recommendations for business researchers.

As a business researcher, it's important to have a clear understanding of the quantitative methods you use in your research. Quantitative methods are essential for making sense of the data you collect and for measuring the impact of your research. In this subchapter, we'll offer some final thoughts and recommendations to help you make the most of your quantitative research.

First, it's important to understand the limitations of quantitative research. While quantitative methods are powerful tools for analyzing data, they can only tell you so much. It's essential to use qualitative methods as well to get a more complete picture of the research problem you're investigating.

Second, it's important to be aware of the assumptions that underlie your quantitative research. These assumptions can affect the validity of your results and the conclusions you draw from them. Make sure you're familiar with the assumptions of the statistical tests you use and that you're using appropriate tests for your data.

Third, it's important to be transparent about your research methods. This includes everything from how you collected your data to how you analyzed it. Being transparent allows others to replicate your research and build on it, which is essential for advancing the field of business research.

Fourth, it's important to be mindful of the ethical

implications of your research. This includes protecting the privacy of your research participants, ensuring that they are fully informed about the research, and minimizing any harm that may result from your research.

Finally, we recommend that business researchers stay up-to-date with the latest developments in quantitative research methods. There are always new tools and techniques being developed, and staying on top of these developments can help you improve the quality of your research and stay ahead of the curve in your field.

In conclusion, quantitative methods are essential for business researchers, but it's important to use them wisely. By being aware of the limitations of quantitative research, understanding the assumptions that underlie it, being transparent about your research methods, being mindful of ethical implications, and staying up-to-date with the latest developments, business researchers can conduct high-quality research that advances the field and makes a meaningful impact in the business world.

ABOUT THE AUTHOR

Sales and Marketing Professional with more than 25 Plus years of diversified experience for both transnational and national pharmaceutical companies such as Merck & Co. Inc. NV Organon, AkzoNobel, and OBS Pakistan (Pvt.) Limited. Moreover, he is a university Professor and has more than 10 years' experience of teaching, research and supervising dissertations for MBA, MS. M.Phil., and Ph.D. level students. He is an author and coauthor of more than 200 publications, in which he has written more than 80 impact factor research articles, and 20 books.